Am I a Good FRIEND?

A Book about Trustworthiness

ROBIN NELSON

Lerner Publications Company • Minneapolis

Lerner Publications Company
A division of Lerner Publishing Group, Inc.
241 First Avenue North
Minneapolis, MN 55401 U.S.A.

For reading levels and more information, look up this title at
www.lernerbooks.com.

Library of Congress Cataloging-in-Publication Data

Nelson, Robin, 1971–
    Am I a good friend? : a book about trustworthiness / by Robin Nelson.
        pages   cm. — (Show your character)
    Includes index.
    ISBN 978–1–4677–1361–0 (lib. bdg. : alk. paper)
    ISBN 978–1–4677–2520–0 (eBook)
    Trust—Juvenile literature. 2. Reliability—Juvenile literature.
  3. Friendship—Juvenile literature. I. Title.
    BJ1500.T78N45 2014
    177'.62—dc23   2013026105

Manufactured in the United States of America
1 – MG – 12/31/13

TABLE OF CONTENTS

Can you keep a secret? Do you tell the truth? Do you keep your promises? **Being trustworthy shows people you are a good friend.**

Being trustworthy means you are honest. You do what you say you will do. It means you won't forget or decide to do something else.

A good friend does what is right and honest, even when it seems hard. How can you be a good friend? Let's take a look at some questions and answers about trustworthiness and find out!

Molly told me what she got Ally for her birthday. Molly made me promise to keep it a secret. Ally wants me to tell her what it is. **IS IT OKAY TO BREAK MY PROMISE?**

No!
Being a good friend means keeping your promises.

You promised Molly you wouldn't tell Ally what she got her. **Keep the present a secret.** Tell Ally you promised Molly you wouldn't tell. You could tell Ally she'll love her gift! It will be more fun for Ally if she is surprised.

I asked Ben to play baseball after school, and he said he can't. He said he got in trouble at home for lying to his mom. He asked me not to tell anyone. But our friends want to know why Ben can't come.

SHOULD I TELL MY FRIEND'S SECRET?

No.
Ben asked you not to tell anyone. Telling would be breaking a promise to Ben.

When you break a friend's promise, that friend will feel bad. Your friend also might not trust you anymore. That would make you feel bad. **Just tell your friends Ben can't come today.**

Okay, so I know I shouldn't tell Ben's secret, since Ben asked me not to. But what if Ben hadn't asked me to keep his punishment a secret?

Could I tell my friends then?

No. It would still be a bad idea to tell your friends. It's never okay to tell your friends bad things about anyone.

Trustworthy friends don't talk about one another behind their backs.

Spreading information about other people is gossiping. Gossiping is often mean-spirited. It can hurt people's feelings. Don't spread gossip. If you hear your friends saying mean things about someone else, walk away.

Did You Know?
A lot of gossip isn't even true. Gossip can just be rumors. Spreading rumors is a form of bullying.

When people start gossiping, change the subject or walk away.

No.
A good friend doesn't cancel when something better comes along.

Tell your grandma you already made plans with Ashley. Your grandma will understand. You can play with Ashley today and plan another day to go to the zoo with your grandma.

I borrowed Jake's remote control car. I broke it by accident when I was playing with it. I didn't want Jake to be mad at me, so I told him I didn't do it. But he still won't let me play with his new toy spaceship. WHY WON'T MY FRIEND TRUST ME WITH HIS TOY?

It's hard to **admit when you've done something wrong**. But you should have told Jake you broke his car instead of lying.

Jake might have been mad about the car if you explained what really happened. But he would also know he could trust you to **tell the truth**.

So how can I get Jake to trust me again?

Tell Jake **the truth**. Apologize for breaking his car. You could even offer to buy him a new one.

You also need to **apologize for lying**. Jake might be mad. He might not trust you right away. Be honest with him, and you might earn his trust again.

Apologizing can be difficult. Your friend might be upset by what you have to say. But it is important to tell your friend the truth.

Your friends will be more likely to share their toys with you if they know you are trustworthy.

I like to play jokes on my friends. I tell them we have a pop quiz when we don't. I pretend I'm hurt. I tell them there are snakes on the playground. But today I saw a hornets' nest at the park. My friends didn't believe me, and Jack got stung.

WHY DIDN'T MY FRIENDS BELIEVE ME?

Playing jokes might seem fun to you. **But telling lies makes it hard for others to trust you.**

When you tell stories that aren't true, your friends can't tell when you are playing a joke and when you are telling the truth. When you told them about the hornets' nest, they thought you were joking. Your friends will trust you only if you start telling the truth.

Did You Know?

Have you heard the story "The Boy Who Cried Wolf"? It's about a shepherd boy who lies about a wolf attacking his sheep. Soon a real wolf appears, but no one believes the boy because of all his lies. To "cry wolf" means "to lie about a danger."

That shirt might be one of Maddie's favorites. She might be looking for it. She'll be **so happy** when you give it back to her!

21

Mary and I were playing in her room. We made a big mess. Her mom said she would take us to get ice cream after we cleaned up Mary's room. Mary said we should just put everything under her bed.

IS IT OKAY TO ONLY PRETEND TO CLEAN UP?

No way.

Mary's room might look clean if you hide everything under her bed. But Mary's mom would not like it if she knew you did that.

It isn't honest to be rewarded for doing a job poorly. Be a good, trustworthy friend and guest. Tell Mary you should put everything away where it belongs. With two of you, the job will be done quickly. Then you can really enjoy your ice cream!

Ms. Strand keeps a collection of action figures on her desk. When I walked by it this morning, I took one. Ms. Strand saw it was missing and asked me if I knew who took it. I lied and told her it was Dan. So Dan has to miss recess.

SHOULD I TELL MY TEACHER THE TRUTH?

Being trustworthy means telling the truth **even if you get in trouble**. You need to be honest and stand up for Dan.

If you stand up for Dan, you might have to miss recess. But you will **feel better** if you are honest. And Dan will feel better too!

Your teacher will appreciate that you told her the truth.

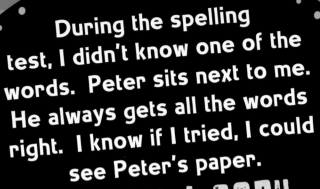

During the spelling test, I didn't know one of the words. Peter sits next to me. He always gets all the words right. I know if I tried, I could see Peter's paper.

SHOULD I COPY MY CLASSMATE'S TEST?

It may seem easy to just copy Peter's paper, but it's not honest. **Being honest isn't easy.** But cheating is wrong, and it will make you feel bad. Keep your eyes on your own paper and **just try your best**.

If you can do the right thing even when it's hard, you will earn the trust of those around you. **Trustworthy people make the best friends.** How will you show your friends you're trustworthy?

TRUSTWORTHY DOS AND DON'TS

Did what you read in this book inspire you to be as trustworthy as you can be? If so, here are a few dos and don'ts for you to follow as you strive to lead a trustworthy life!

Dos

- **Do** keep your promises.

- **Do** what you say you will do.

- **Do** tell the truth.

- **Do** be honest with your words and actions.

- **Do** keep private information private.

- **Do** have the courage to do what is right.

Don'ts

· **Don't** lie.

· **Don't** cheat.

· **Don't** steal.

· **Don't** say things that could hurt others.

· **Don't** do things that could hurt others.

· **Don't** trick anyone.

Can you think of any other trustworthy dos and don'ts?

apologize: to say you are sorry

bullying: making someone feel hurt, afraid, or uncomfortable over and over again

cheating: doing something dishonest to gain an advantage. For example, if you copied a classmate's answers to get a better grade, you would be cheating.

copy: to write something down exactly as it is somewhere else

gossiping: spreading information about other people

honest: good and truthful

rumor: a story that has been passed from person to person but might not be true

stealing: taking something that does not belong to you

trustworthy: trusted to be honest and to do what you say you will do

FURTHER INFORMATION

Donovan, Sandy. *How Can I Deal with Bullying? A Book about Respect*. Minneapolis: Lerner Publications, 2014. There's a lot more to bullying than gossip and rumors. Read about what to do if you experience bullying.

Gossip and Rumors: Did You Hear?
http://pbskids.org/itsmylife/friends/rumors
Learn about what rumors and gossip really are and how you can stop them from doing damage to you and your friends.

Greve, Meg. *Integrity*. Vero Beach, FL: Rourke, 2012. While enjoying the colorful photos in this book, find out what it means to have integrity.

Raatma, Lucia. *Trustworthiness*. Ann Arbor, MI: Cherry Lake Publishing, 2013. This is an easy-to-read book with real-world examples of trustworthiness.

Roberts, Cynthia. *Honesty*. Chanhassen, MN: Child's World, 2008. Find out what it means to be honest.

LERNER SOURCE™
Expand learning beyond the printed book. Download free, complementary educational resources for this book from our website, www.lerneresource.com.

PHOTO ACKNOWLEDGMENTS

The images in this book are used with the permission of: © Christopher Futcher/E+/Getty Images, p. 4; © Blend Images/Shutterstock.com, p. 5; © Sergiyn/Dreamstime.com, p. 6; © Jade/Blend Images/Getty Images, p. 7; © PhotoAlto/Sigrid Olsson/The Agency Collection/Getty Images, p. 9; © iStockphoto.com/GlobalStock/Vetta Collection, p. 10; © Speedo101/Dreamstime.com, p. 11; © Kidstock/Blend Images/Getty Images, p. 12; © Digital Vision/Thinkstock, p. 13; © Isabelle Rozenbaum/PhotoAlto SAS/Alamy, p. 15; © Photodisc/Digital Vision/Getty Images, p. 16; © Ryan McVay/Lifesize/Getty Images, p. 17; © Canettistock/Dreamstime.com, p. 19; © iStockphoto.com/Pepifoto, p. 20; © Anatols/Dreamstime.com, p. 21; © Henglein and Steets/cultura/CORBIS, p. 22; © Ranplett/E+/Getty Images, p. 23; © Myrleen Pearson/Alamy, p. 25; © Kidstock/BlendImagesAlamy, p. 26; © Hemera/Thinkstock, p. 27.

Front cover: © George Doyle/Stockbyte/Getty Images.

Main body text set in ChurchwardSamoa Regular. Typeface provided by Chank.